WE ARE THE ROSES

A collection of inspirational readings

Written by

Francisco Guerra

Independently published by

Francisco Guerra

ISBN: 9798860202269

We are always learning how to be strong. We thrive through the shadows of misfortune. We were not created to be powerless and unwise. We were created to be victorious in every mold. But it is through the storms that we learn the tide. We learn to harden our efforts and survive daringly with firmness on our shoulders and boldness in our eyes. It is in our best interest to always allow the space between where we are and where we want to be, to advance us in the direction of our purpose. We are the epitome of growth, the evolution of self.

We are the roses, blooming from darkness.

Contents

SPROUTING

Every day you are in transformation. You are shedding old pieces of yourself and giving birth to new ones. During this - you may feel challenged and discouraged. Practice self-compassion as an essential part of this growth. Be easy on yourself. Pour a little faith into discovering every natural part of this transition. Always remember - Growth and comfort can never coexist.

It's so important to surround yourself with people that will help you advance. Life moves forward. It will never make sense to take steps backwards. Attachment can become detrimental to your growth. Be careful who and what you cling to. Find the courage to renounce the things that no longer serve your purpose. Be brave in letting go. You will see the universe pay you back in unimaginable ways.

Never feel guilty for rearranging your goals. We go through constant changes and sometimes our purpose and outlook on life need to be adapted. You may not be the same person you were last year. You might have learned new things and experienced a different type of freedom. Abandon old plans with ease and confidence. Continue growing and embrace change as a way to discover new beginnings.

You will be okay.

It becomes so easy, almost second nature, for us to point fingers when we feel unaccomplished. We project our own insecurities onto others by blaming them for the times we fall short or have setbacks. That is not a recipe for growth. We have to be accountable for our own actions. Our successes are results of what we do and in some cases what we *don't* do. Find clarity in mindfulness, find peace in acceptance, and find truth in honesty. You will be liberated in your efforts. Trust yourself.

Do not be dismayed by mistakes. When massed
with personal understanding, it can be the spark
plug you need to find your true self.
Disappointment, failure, and disheartenment are
the tools the universe will hurl your way to
guide you in all your graceful mending. Do not
be so high handed in your wisdom. It's wise to
be cautioned that the strongest of us may
dwindle and the wisest might miscalculate. Do
not allow pride to meddle in your journey. A
good person knows when their unfolding is
wrong. It's important that you can forgive
yourself and repair the harm done. This
will empower you beyond measure.

Life is not infallible - however, we grow through experience and understanding. That is the beauty of existence. Growing is living. Be gentle with yourself. The sincerest evidence of life is growth. They say we find the greatest opportunities outside our comfort zone. Challenge yourself to dive deep into those waters. Let the restless fear of not having all the answers bring you a sense of surrender, which in turn, will be the catalyst to everything wonderful you have to offer.

Remember to be kind to yourself. Speak life into your thoughts and cultivate a place of peace. Self-love is imperative to sustain worthy thoughts. Acknowledge that you are deserving of the same love you tender to others. Keep guard of your body, mind, and heart. Stay true to your spirit without misgiving. Life is determined to disclose your true self at some point. Be ready for that revelation. Give yourself the grace and freedom to elevate your purpose. Always treat yourself accordingly and do not lapse into a realm of guilt just because you make yourself the priority. Set the standard on how you invite the world in. You too, are important.

Do not drain yourself with things unworthy of your energy. Prioritize where your efforts spill. You are deserving of so much love and encouragement. Dedicate time to the people who inspire and uplift you. Eliminate those who only want to extract from you. It's important to know when to shut the door. If you are drained, then you have no room to give. Don't allow unworthy people to leave footprints in your mind. Negative people will always look for a new place to dump their trash.

Don't let that place be you.

The beauty in falling is the fortuitous occurrence of genuine discovery. Only by failure do we appreciate the need to reset, refocus and amend our faults. Failure is an essential part of your journey to success. It's imperative to heed the lessons of the disappointments and hardships. Embrace all the opportunities that come with failure. Take every loss as a single defeat and not as the final bout. Do not be afraid to fail miserably. It will be your steppingstone to achieve greatly. It may even be necessary to encounter these defeats. It will show you who you truly are and what you're capable of overcoming.

Not everyone has the same heart as you. It's inevitable that people will disappoint you. We sometimes create our own heartbreak through what we expect from people. Seems the more loyal you are, the more you see how selfish people can be. It's hard to not let these things affect you, so take it with grace the best way you can and continue to smile.

You can never be true to yourself by pleasing others. People pleasing comes with a false sense of contentment. It only feels gratifying until all your efforts just seem desperate and restless. You will ultimately lose people in your journey through life, but it's considerably important to not lose yourself in the process. Always come from a place of kindness but without reservations that will cause you regret or resentment later on. Be compassionate and empathize with others but don't bear the pressure of trying to rescue people all the time. Always remember, when you say "yes" to others, make sure you're not saying "no" to yourself.

Sometimes you have to make yourself a priority.
Save enough water for yourself. There is a
reason you outgrow people. Those who
do you wrong, leave no room for malevolence.

Learn to leave the bad where it sits.

Embrace yourself in full length. Show up in all your missteps just as much as you show up in all your splendor. This world will be keen on casting judgment on you just as fast as you can speak. It will continually remind you of all your shortcomings. This is where you have to focus on the things you do have. Focus on everything that makes you exceptional. Rebound your thoughts and echo everything you have to offer. You will see that everything you love about yourself will always be enough.

Celebrating your successes is unquestionably noteworthy. It's paramount for growth and significant for self-confidence. However, to heed the lessons of failure is how you sustain solid character. The beauty of defeat is that there will most likely be an opportunity to realign and make the changes necessary to try again. Always meet your failures as the bigger person. View failure as a steppingstone towards all the greatness life has in store for you. Never be so cautious with life, that you fail by default. Have acceptance in knowing that you won't always make the right decisions - and in understanding this rule, it will inordinately contribute to your success.

Be comfortable with shattering pieces of yourself in order to reconstruct. There is no timeline for your soul. You will die countless deaths and be plunged into reinvention many times. In moments of disharmony, do not abandon your efforts, instead find ways to realign your purpose and continue finding yourself. Nothing has to be permanent. You can completely learn yourself over and over again. Revitalize your passion, recollect your spirit, and begin reclaiming your life.

Self-awareness is a balance of knowing your strengths and your weaknesses. There is a solitary freedom to gain in the process of discovering every part of yourself. Everything you think that disturbs your peace is in reality leading you to a better understanding of yourself. When you try to look outward, your vision just becomes a fleeting reverie, but when you look inward, that is where a true awakening befalls. All the answers you seek are at the center of your being. We are - what we mostly hide. Have the courage to look at yourself honestly, but gently. Accept yourself as you are and then you can compose change, that is the inquisitive paradox of life.

The ultimate confidence one can have is knowing how to keep your own pace. Don't allow this world to scurry your efforts. Maintain a genuine posture even through the haste that this world often brings. Forward is forward, so keep moving. There is no advantage to propelling your way through life. Your understanding and awareness must take place little by little. Phase out all expectations of where you "think" you're supposed to be in life. Embrace your pace in your journey. There are no rules. Your quest may look different, but it's yours to call your own. Remember that.

"Once you open your mouth, you tell the world who you are"

With this undertaking, we must be mindful of what our words harvest in the spirit of expression. The words we use and the way we speak are the essence of who we are deep inside. We are masters of what we lull on our tongue. Once conveyed to the world, we become its captive. Safeguard your tongue as you would any revered possession. One word could bring dishonor to your name. Be waveless and ponder. Speak with integrity and always be precise with your words. Only give it direction of love and truth.

It may be a hard-won battle to
not be dismayed at living broken. Whatever
heartbreak or grief has cornered your spirit, let
light shine on every feeling that spurts from the
unfavorable moments that come. Invite the
healing process as a passageway
to believe a change is coming for
the better. It's also important to understand that
even when you heal, you will not be the same
person you were before. But with a little thing
called grace, like water - it will flow to the
lowest parts of us and fill us with newborn
purpose and softly eliminate all shame.

Become absorbed with the idea that your season of change is on the way. Everything that you desire is headed for your grasp. Everywhere you want to be is gently anticipating your happening. Relinquish all old energy in things of the past. Focus on building something new, something bold, something beautiful. Welcome every new feeling that is stirring inside of you. Fence off the idea that we must only endure life. Start living it! Keep going in the direction of your dreams. Bloom in all things that make your heart happy and free.

Do not be discouraged by the subtle growth that cultivates in your life. Your wins will not always be emphatic and boastful. Now and again, growth will come in a hushed nature, and just because it's not prominent in your acknowledgment, it does not mean it is insignificant. Your growth is measured by a multitude of things, and not solely based on what you display for the world to see. Continue to grow silently and embellish the power of silence that will at long last bring you a sense of understanding and purpose.

It's imperative that you do not dwell on the bad days. No matter how rugged and unyielding they may feel, they serve as a catalyst for all things that serve your purpose. Ease the pressure and concern of feeling you have to problem solve everything. You don't always have the answers and that's okay. Acknowledge your good days as happiness and accept your bad days as experience. At minimum, your worst days will hold invaluable lessons. Sometimes the best thing we can do is just survive. You are still in control. Breathe, and begin to regain your power in remembering who you are and who you choose to be.

Conformity should never be an inflated thought. Discovering the essential you is a delightful way to always be yourself. Allow people to see your unfeigned imperfections. Certainly, it's better to be absolutely preposterous than absolutely lifeless. Allow change to take its course, but never to the point of scaling down your worth. Be an element of strength that shields all your hardships. Your expression is unique. There is an imprudent life force we must draw from to truly be at peace. Remain steady amongst the haste of life, live your truth tacitly but undoubtedly. The essence of your vitality will breathe through your actions, but if you deter, it will be lost in existence. Be who you are, unashamed.

Some of your best moments are around the corner. With some subtle changes, you can begin living a life of intelligible truth. No matter how minuscule the change, you can clench considerable favor towards your destiny. You may even find solace in considering alternatives. Use fresh eyes to nourish new patterns. Life will never gridlock the inevitable. Don't resist the series of spontaneous changes that come into being. Learn to change your mind without the guilt trip. Stop swimming in safeguarded ponds and start capturing the ocean that is desperate for your push.

There is a rebellion that lives deep inside all of us. The kind that guides you into loving yourself in the open, spontaneous, and with such pealing of the heart. This junction to your name is admirable and praiseworthy. Make sure you celebrate it as such. Fall in love with the work in progress you are but also breathe joyance in the beautiful work of art you already are. Yes, you can be both. This world will try to undermine your value and eradicate the light that you are. Life is a journey of boundless horizons. Accept yourself in the unexampled mold that you are. Love yourself, and always, always move forward.

It will always be such an enchanting journey trying to understand your heart. It breathes into reason of its own. It feels everything, and yet understands nothing solidly. But whilst on this discovery, get to know your heart. It will always discern what the mind isn't ready for. Listen to every beat. Listen above the clattery. Embrace every sound candidly. Let it guide you into worlds of opportunities and corners of success. Remain true without reserve. Your heart is life's most honest road map. Follow it in full view, blatantly. Keep exploring. Live this experience of life naturally, and even when you think that's it –

PUSH B E Y O N D.

The scars that adorn your soul, are calmly primed to be embraced by your compassion. Once you learn to love your scars, you will manifest beauty throughout every strand of your brokenness. Through the cracks of your unpleasantness, is where light will find a way to brush your hurt. In essence, to usher in such compassion and empathy when you're down and out, is one of the most genuine signs of strength. We are all broken in contrasting ways. No matter the level of parallel, we all divvy from the same condition. Sometimes, it takes being broken to find yourself whole again.

Build with people who aren't afraid to grow.
Frame your intentions with a sense of clarity.
Invest your energy wisely. Surround
yourself with those who inspire and challenge
you to elevate your ground. When you're
around people that make you feel calm and
radiant, then you're in the right place. Time will
eventually decide who sets foot in your life, your
heart will mediate who belongs in your life, and
you will then ordain who stays in your life. Be
brave enough to let go of those who weigh you
down. When you align with the right people -
life will color you brilliantly.

Speak kindly to yourself. You have survived
wars some don't even know about. Give
yourself more credit for the battles you have
won. The self-criticism is not constructive.
Applaud yourself more and witness change take
place. Harvest mercy on your own soul. You are
always listening to yourself in your mind, so
make it commendatory. Extend compassion and
kindness to yourself. Stay truthful to your spirit,
unerring in your actions and never doubt what
you're capable of. Breathe deeply, let your mind
sail to the moon. Life is steadfast in showing
you who you truly are. Capture it. Embrace it.
Claim the unique power you have to heal your
life.

Learn to have a place with your feelings. You don't always have to feel like they need to be unloaded. Most times, it only leads to spaces that feel hollow. A lot of people will acknowledge you, but will they truthfully try to understand you? You are worthy of being engrossed with love and compassion. The energy you carry is remarkable and unprecedented. Your feelings are noteworthy and well founded. You deserve to be heard in every stretch of truth. So, before you surge into the world with the weight of your heart, always remember - no one hears you louder than you.

The irony of heartbreak is that it also comes with a reserved clarity. It will enlighten your self-worth, therefrom edifying a multitude of reasons to seize your own happiness. It will serve as an earmarked opportunity to heal, evolve, and also emerge with a stronger capacity to love. The unfortunate event of heartbreak is best embraced as an imminent human experience. Focus inward and entwine yourself with every silver lining that comes with heartbreak. We will never be able to control what comes, or how it chooses to leave. However, we can take in arms every bit of beauty that our hearts want to enfold and cherish what we have while it's here.

In life, there are times we have to make tracks
for the uncomfortable pain to show its form.
True growth is not meant to be slight, on the
contrary, it is meant to stir the deepest
challenges that will make you want to relinquish
all efforts. In this, you will grow immensely.
Keep in mind, mishaps are essential to the
process of your greatest discovery. Your
personal unfolding depends largely on it.
Always stay the course. Transitional
stages are often necessary but can also leave you
susceptible and unguarded. Practice patience and
always be gentle with yourself.

Your days will not always be cheerful and lighthearted. You will have days that seem appalling and hard to take patiently. Come what may, continue to lean into the light. Always keep going, even more so when it is easier said than done. Break off any doubt that drapes in your mind. There is a process to attain sureness in your spirit. The mission should always be growth. Give yourself the freedom to heal and readjust when need be. Always remember, things don't happen to us, they happen for us.

Take a step back and reflect. Acknowledge that there is still ample room for you to continue growing in all the ways you were meant to. One of the most honest transformations comes from pulsating out of your realm of comfort.

We are all guilty of carrying a sense of discontent that plants the seed of urgency, that makes us want to explore something different. Be headstrong in the choices you make, spring from curiosity, allow it to lead you to better life decisions. Never become attached to this frivolous world. It is ever changing. Something new is always in the wind. Follow your heart, but always adapt accordingly.

There is an unseen version of yourself that you haven't met yet. You see, as time expands into all corners of the earth, we grow just as such, in extensive ways. It's important to believe that only your best version is in the making. The past versions of you only carry lessons and tears, both which have garnished that smile on your face because you survived what you thought would shatter you. Every version you illustrate of yourself is a collage of what it takes to revive yourself and remain anchored to your destiny. You will continue to form into everything that is meant for you. Your best version is on the horizon. Live for it.

Find amenity in your season of change and maturation. Progress is hardly made if there is fear in your heart. Change can be intimidating; it can cause insecurity to parade its disquieted ways. I believe that any change, especially one that is abetted by uneasiness, can certainly make a genuine impact on your life. Embrace all corners of it. Live in the splendor of ambiguity. You will never be disenchanted by what the universe has aligned for you. This is your season of change. The eminence of everything you are destined to be. Everything is happening beautifully. Trust it.

You cannot conform to a level of comfort with expectations to grow. Both of these things will never exist in the same space in your life. Your comfort zone is a safe place to be, but it crushes your courage and dismantles your confidence. Without challenge, you may lose a beautiful opportunity for something great to change you for the better. All the great things you will find on the other side of your comfort zone. Free yourself from the psychological state of familiarity, safety, and security. In the end, it will be rewarding and fulfilling, all because you broke through.

People come, and people go. Some visit for a while, others make a home in our heart. Some cheer for you, some stand back to see if you fail. It's ok to outgrow people. It's bad enough to be complacent with life itself - don't become complacent with the company you keep. Some are just here for the lessons, and the ones that truly matter will be the ones to remember and hold dear. Never feel guilty for leaving unnecessary people behind. If they aren't growing with you, excuse yourself and keep it moving. Life is not here for understanding. Life is here to live in your purpose.

Do that - faithfully.

Find the courage today to accept all things for
what they are. Find understanding in the things
that make you uneasy. Cease the expectations
and advance yourself with gratitude in your
heart. Acceptance is always the first step to
attaining a peaceful mindset. It's always easier
said than done because we want full control of
our lives. Try not to lose yourself in your
emotions because you will not win that
battle. There is true wisdom in
knowing the difference between having peace in
what you cannot change and showing prowess in
what you can change.

Change can sometimes be erratic. It can be intimidating. It can cause unsettled waters that make you feel uneasy. Accept that challenge in a constructive way. It will help renew your confidence. Uncertainty- when embraced the right way, can be the ultimate blessing. Adjust and fasten your desire to be great. Change can be good. Maintain perspective and keep your heart centered in all things that bring you happiness.

That same smile you give to a stranger - make sure it finds you as well. That hug you give your closest friends - make sure you save one for you as well. That laughter you share in the best moments - make sure to laugh at yourself too. We carry so much weight of all the things we offer this world - and yet, most of us are empty inside. Don't allow this world to drain you to the point that you forget to pour into yourself. You are important, and you must be gentle with yourself. Be kind to yourself. All the good that you want to bring to the world - bring it to yourself first. That isn't selfish. It's making sure you're full of everything first before you have the capacity to give.

Say what you feel. Say what you need to say. No matter how difficult or uncomfortable. The best forms of healing are when you open yourself up.

Sometimes in life you need to pause and
observe. It's hard to bite your tongue
when you have so much passion inside you. It's
hard to turn the other cheek. It's hard to seem
unbothered. People will test every part
of you to bring you out of character. If you lose
faith in people, the best thing to do is just take
notice, and learn to maneuver
differently. You have to protect your peace of
mind at all costs.

With some honest self-reflection, we can see the darkest parts of us that need healing. Never be ashamed of the incomplete you. We are all a work in progress. I don't believe we are ever fully complete, nor do I believe we should be. Life is a marathon. We race, but the finish line is irrelevant. Just keep going. Don't stop to see if you're winning. Your wins will come. But take the time to bear your losses. That is where you gain understanding. That is where you gain wisdom. Losing is essential to becoming the best version of yourself. When you lose with grace - you learn the true value of your wins.

It's ok to unplug from the world sometimes.
Disconnect in a constructive way and you will
boast a refined sense of purpose. You will find
new energy and a new
perspective. Our minds and bodies become
cluttered and demanding after so many days of
challenges and obstacles. Detach yourself
temporarily and feel confident that you will
return a better you in the long run.

We may think that we have wasted our time in one form or another during our lives in certain situations. However, the perspective should be - we once dedicated that time to something we believed in. Good or bad in the end, it taught us something valuable. As the saying goes, we live and learn. So never think that time was lost. Time is always given, and no matter how it plays out. We are better today - because we lived and because we learned.

A new week is upon us. We are here,
we are alive. Let us be grateful in our journey.
Keep embracing the good and the bad.
It's all a part of our progression to becoming the
version of ourselves that we ultimately want to
be. Keep growing. Keep smiling. Keep every
feeling that brings you joy close to your heart.
Every day is a step closer to everything you have
your heart set on. Don't stop believing.

The goal should always be to be better, not perfect. Don't hold yourself to an image of perfection that will never exist. Don't be hard on yourself when setbacks occur. It's all a part of your progression. There will be difficult roads, and vigorous obstacles, but stay the course. Cease your expectations and always be proud of how far you've come. Do your best and give credit for your sincerest efforts.

You owe it to yourself.

Often, especially during trying times, we ask God for strength. We ask for the courage to surmount all adversity. We ask for patience in the process. I strongly believe our god is a favorable god. But God does not give us strength without difficulty. God does not give us courage without tribulation. God does not give us patience without uncertainty. Do not become discouraged by unfortunate news or circumstances. When it rains, it pours. See it as a spiritual cleansing. When the sun shines, it radiates. Embrace the glory. Be kind to one another. We're all fighting out here. It's a never-ending war. But every day is worth living. We all have a story. Make yours worth reading.

You may feel that there are people in your life
that owe you apologies. Even if that reigns true,
it will never be as important as the apologies
that you owe to yourself. Guilt will
drain you and hamper any hope of moving
forward. Love yourself enough to know
that you are the provenance of so many beautiful
things that this world needs. Through all the bad
decisions and lack of understanding - your
willingness to grow from it all, is what truly
matters.

You are brave. So brave, for always taking that first step towards your next breakthrough. Never knowing what will materialize on the other side. However, do not be misguided, bravery does not mean you are downright fearless. Bravery comes with a sense of courage, fortitude, and firmness to be able to combat the toughest times of your life. The brave, more often than not, are afraid, but they accept the challenge of overcoming. So, smile in the face of misfortune, harvest strength from all the calamity, and begin to grow in the virtue of your splendid valor.

Honor the moments in your life. The favorable ones just as much as the gloomy ones. They all serve as a catalyst to your foundation, which is rooted in faith and resilience. There are no ordinary moments in your life. Appreciate everything that happens. You need to decide - do you define the moments, or do the moments define you. Always do your best when the moment calls. Reassure yourself of everything you are capable of. Eliminate self-judgment and regret from your plate. Your life is eager to delight in every moment you have. Value your time, treasure it. Appreciate everything for what it is.

With all due respect to your journey, shape your best self, with biddable patience, and welcoming compassion. Do not believe yourself to be vain or selfish. In loving yourself, you realize you are actually unbreakable. There is no real etiquette to growth. You can be unkempt and still be close to being well balanced. Be yours before anyone else's. Self-love is a great shift that establishes your ultimate sense of worth. Set the tone today and fall in love with the process. Seize the sanctuary that rests in your heart. That is your truest home.

Do not spend your life trying to be seen or outlined by other people's perception of you. When others don't acknowledge you, it is not because you lack relevance, it is because they choose to not embellish in your light. Keep shining congruent to your truths. Endorsement from others is short lived in most cases, so focus on the betterment of all things inside you. At the end of the day, despite the chink in one's armor, you are deserving of musing your highest self.

Try not to be so rapt with chasing perfection.
We often believe that mistakes or missteps are
adverse, when in reality, the blunder of your
misfortune should be held in high observation.
Accept the calamity of the disruption inside
your soul. Steps backwards
are not to be muddled or misconceived. The best
part of your journey - is not having all the
answers. Nobody has it all figured out. You
are not ahead or behind; you are in process. True
understanding of this sentiment will allow you
the freedom to bend in ways unimaginable.

Take joy in your unfolding.

SEEDING

Accountability is not the most revivifying thing to accept, be that as it may, it is essential to our personal development. Sometimes, we have to be wrong to evince improvement. We must take responsibility for mistakes that we make, amid our greatest efforts. Through accountability - you will learn mindfulness, acknowledgement, candor, and courage. You are in control of how you present yourself to the world.
Take accountability - this will not only foster trust with others, but it will help you steadily grow into your best self.

Our words are an extension of us. Be mindful of the energy they withhold. Always listen with an inquiring mind. Speak valiantly honestly. Be gentle with your heart, you are always in the process of becoming. Life is abrupt and hasty, but it never flounders at showing you your true self. Our words are fastened with what we believe our reality to be. Affirm beautiful things with your words. Understand the capacity of what our words can elevate, link that with steadfast positivity and behold the abundance it brings.

Fall in love with the journey first. Embrace the process of learning and developing your character to discover who you truly are. There is a waveless beauty in becoming. There is a purposeful space to inhabit between where you are now and where you are going. Life is about accepting challenges, it comes roaring in with extreme defiance, but you must always choose to keep moving forward. Find joy in the small things that at first glance seem trivial. You are a traveler of this thing called life, so put a smile on your face, keep your eyes open to new adventures and without exception, keep filling your heart with all that is deserved.

Life is always a process of becoming. There is a quiet death that exists when we inhabit dormancy. Do not fail by residing in such lifeless waters. Our destiny expands in proportion to everything we believe in.

Friendships and family are not complex. At some point it becomes straightforward and pronounced as to who really cares. People you've known for months will sometimes treat you better than the people you've known for years. It comes with the injunction of life. Be careful who you share your energy with and be careful who you interlace with. People will hate you for the myriad of reasons they make up in their mind. Just be yourself. Be kind and bring light to this rapacious world. Express empathy and compassion. Surviving can be tenacious enough, so don't be an asshole.

Embrace things naturally. Grant them the notion to unravel gracefully. When things come without pressure, you will discern beautiful outcomes. Exercise patience as you keep your feet planted, grounded and present in all your endeavors. Gratitude will be the framework to your destiny. Everything you desire is already within you. It is polished with a sense of wonder and refined with purpose. Your genuine efforts will bloom accordingly and organically. Conjure the most fascinating groundwork your life can spawn.

Free yourself from the burden of people pleasing. Accept everything you are and concede that to be enough.

Do not allow judgement to carry so much weight over you. No one ever really knows fully the wars going on in your life. What they think is nothing for you to take heed of. Let them judge, let them get the wrong impression, let them douse themselves in their meddling. You must remain unique in your power, maintain your integrity. People will filter you through their own lenses. Do not lose sway of the dynamic. You're at no obligation to convince anyone of anything. Certain people will draft their own ideas of how you're supposed to live your life, but trust me, there's no mystery, that life is so much better when you are who you say you are.

It's important to never feel alone. This world can create such a perturbed setting and cause such restless anxiety. The biggest key to sanity is having real friends. As rare as it is, to genuinely have someone in your corner, it is such a priceless gift to bear. Real friends are a prominent connection to life, and they are essential to your road ahead. But stay shy of those who flatter when all is well. True friends will appreciate the deep-seated peculiarities you possess. They will find value in your loopholes. Not in the least, should you ever view friendship as convenience. It is a sweet responsibility that we must mirror with our own actions.

When you grant so much
of yourself, you find yourself depleted and
hollow. Being a people pleaser is a parlous
game. Your authentic self will be
handicapped. Your goals will be empty handed,
and your integrity will be impaired. Be careful
with the habit of trying to make everybody
happy. It only feels good until it becomes
imprudent. Walk away from those destitute of
vision, for they will never see your true worth.
There is power in saying "no" and it will leave
ample space for a momentous "yes". Allow
people to feel the pressure of who you really are
and let them act accordingly.

Cultivate patience during your inner storms. Create breathing space between what you feel and what is happening around you. Do not aim your transgressions carelessly. Do not rush into commotion, it will miscarry your true intentions. If you whirl yourself into things, you will squander readily. The art of gentleness is strength governing control. It is the ability to remain placid, no matter how the river flows. Life is a cycle of calm and chaos. Compose peace of mind as your grand design and frame your life around it. And with this clarity, you will find serenity where you need it most - in your heart.

An intimate love will never take away from your existing measure of greatness. In fact, it will cast more layers of abundance to the beauty that already lives inside you. If you find yourself changing parts of you to furnish someone else's expectations, then you are steadily marching down the road of desertion. Embrace the love that embraces you. The love that tight grips your darkest parts. The love that sees your singularity as something to delight in. The love that holds guard against your direct imperfections. That kind of love is extraordinary, unique, remarkable and captures the essence of what we stay alive for.

A whole new world will be unbarred as you discover and establish empathy and imagination. Empathy grows as we embrace one another and continue to learn. If we have the capacity for the adverse, then we should never halt at the crossing for empathy. It is here that we undertake a community of action. It is here that we begin to see the outset for change. Frame yourself to be delicate with the youth, have wide compassion for the aged, thoughtful of those with intention, and forbearing of the powerless. At some point, you will live in the mold of one of these.

Where one can be intimate with generosity, that is where love shines the most. A helping hand will always be rewarded with refinement. If you can give - GIVE. Exercise your heart in helpful ways. Lift those up who desperately need assistance. In vice versa, surrender to the compass of generosity and always be thankful with a genuine heart. A true badge of compassion is helping someone who may never have the capacity to make restitution. Never be blatant with your goodwill. True kindness comes from understated gestures that move mountains. The irony of giving is that it possesses so much to receive.

Our modest connections in the microscopic ground, is the inception to the impact we can create in the macro landscape. We all carry an earmarked energy that has the power to affect tremendously. Be mindful of how you treat people, how you talk to them. Whether it be your closest friends or causal strangers. Be someone who will declare peace in other hearts, so they may always feel supported and heard. This world isn't so bad when you help someone feel seen and acknowledged. Be someone that will help see the good in this world. Be the light in shaded corners. Be the breath of fresh air. Make this place less scary for someone that just wants to feel alive.

Embrace the detours in your life. They are delicate blessings waiting to overlay you with a deeper understanding of where you're headed. It can be empowering to think you are off track but you're actually on the path to your greatest destination. The detours in life will be limitless, endless, and constant. Learn to adore the process. Life is swift and eager. It will heave you into dark places and moments of anguish. When things aren't going your way, do not become crimped with frustration or impatience. Life's lessons often come disguised as an alternate route. Do not be afraid of the detour. It is meant for you.

There is a grand picture of all things cultivating in your life. We don't always understand why we experience certain situations, but nonetheless we must believe we are headed somewhere pure and just. I strongly believe things work out in our favor, and we must relinquish all things we can't control and trust in the bigger picture. Trust in this and you will feel your heart swell with an abundance of hope. Uncertainty may hold a sense of dubiety, but the ultimate prize here, is recognizing that faith will conquer all. You will be okay, and life will be on your side. Trust it to ground all great things in your favor.

Tears - A beautiful waterfall of grace. When our hearts can't contain the emotion, our tears do the talking. Whether it be from pain, loss, or joy, our tears can be the perfect canvas of what we are feeling inside. The irony - that tears are so weightless but yet feel so heavy on our hearts. Learn to find comfort in your tears. It is never a sign of weakness. It can be freeing in so many aspects. Never be ashamed to weep. If your heart needs to breathe, give it that freedom. Mute your tongue. Let your eyes do the talking. Feel it all. It's a cleanse worthy of so many blessings.

Life is pretty practical. You bring good to the world; the universe will find a way to double all its goodness in your favor. Be an example of love. Be compassionate. Be a voice of encouragement. Be the smile someone needs to see to brighten their day. Be the laughter someone needs to hear to bring light back into their life. Be the helping hand they need to reach the finish line. Just be a good person. Be someone that breaks the cycle. Make a promise to yourself to always be better than the things that broke you, so that you may always come from a place of love and understanding and never from your pain.

To life's utter dismay, there are many insecure people that surround us every day. Some are the ones we hold very close, and others come in the form of acquaintances. You have to be careful of who is really on your side. Very few are genuinely happy to see you win. This is why it's so important that you're completely invested in yourself. Don't get caught up with who is in your corner. Have faith in yourself and those who aren't meant to be at your side in your glory, you will find them there.

There is a misconception about being soft
in a world that makes you feel inadequate
because of it. Being soft does not hinder your
strength. It does not make you any less
powerful. On the contrary - to be
soft is a courageous act that radiates
compassion and love. Something that the
world is in desperate need of. There is a constant
ego check happening in this world, every day.
We are consumed by things that make
us appear a certain way, when in reality, only
represents a false notion of what we want others
to think. I believe we are all softer than what we
parade. We would all rather be loved than hated.
We would all rather be hugged than
pushed away.
Being soft also means being strong. This is a
rare bravery in mastering that combination.

Compassion is the ultimate gift one can bestow
to the world. It hauls a sense of nobility and
brings warmth to the soul. If you can be
anything in this world - be kind.

Every bad situation doesn't last forever. Time helps heal, eventually. There will always be room for new opportunity. You are worth more than you can even begin to imagine. Trust the process of all your hardships. Trust the rain when it asks you to get wet. Trust the pain when it asks you to hurt. Trust the tears when they ask you to feel. Trust the pieces of your heart to become whole again. You will make it out of the darkness. Keep the faith.

When other people leave you hollow, take that as a blessing to begin filling yourself with more of YOU. All the time that you have been left broken, those scattered pieces were unnecessary weight that now, you no longer have to bear. It will forever reign true, that we must accept the fall, to be able to learn our capacity to fly. We all deserve light upon our skin, but first you must love yourself out of darkness.

One day it's all going to make sense.
The part we live is just life's interlude. However, we must show our truth, without provision. We must retreat from the lies that this world tries to convey. Walk on the path of goodwill and graciousness. This universe will always align with your purpose and assist you in carrying out the process. So, when the time comes to understand the paradox of life, you can say with an honest heart, that you played your part.

If there ever comes a time for separation, whether it be with people or places - make sure you leave satisfied knowing that you gave the best parts of yourself. Knowing that you never assisted halfheartedly. Knowing that through the good and bad, you stuck it through with good intentions. Leave calmly with ease in your heart, knowing that you played your part the best you could.

So often we are so focused on rising to the top - all with good reason, of course. However, did you find lessons in the failures? Did you find a new perspective when the world seemed to have blocked your blessings? What did you gain from the fall? Because in all retrospect - How you put yourself back together through disruption, is a true testament to the perseverance you carry inside you. Don't be ashamed of your setbacks. There will soon be an overflow of joy when time aligns your heart once again with your purpose.

Stay inspired.

I ask that you live. That you love. That you value every moment that comes into your space. Every person, the permanent things, and the temporary things. Find the magic in every chapter of your life. Every day, in the good, the bad, and the ugly. In all the laughter, and in all the tears. Never carry fear in your heart. Align your heart with grace, and live free.

It's important to be mindful of how we react to things. Not everything calls for your attention. However, never embalm your emotions. Speak your mind when necessary. Don't allow the negative things to provoke you. The things that occur will never be as important as how you choose to react to them. Practice stillness within your spirit. There is an immense power in not reacting. Center yourself and remain thoughtful with your intentions.

Sometimes you have to be careful about being the peaceful one. People will bemuse your intentions. They will see you as passive and frail. The challenge is to remain placid in moments of turmoil. A calm mind will be one of your greatest weapons once you master it. It will be your inner guide to achieve the clarity you need to manifest the perfect balance of consciousness. There is always strength in stillness - capture it.

Life can be very consuming and enthralling. However, you should never have to ask someone for their time, love, attention, happiness, or respect. Those things must come from a genuine place, and never by obligation. You must love yourself enough to never have to seek these things from other people. Inconsistency is a dangerous thing. Distance yourself from mediocre people who are threatened by your strength. You will see when darkness comes to light, who is really on your side - Pay attention.

Letting go is not always about losing something. In many ways, it can be such a fortunate gain. When you let go of what no longer serves you, you begin to discover a new space for new beginnings. Holding on to toxicity will only hinder the hope of renewing your life for the better. Unsubscribe to the people who dim your light. They don't deserve the thought of you. Let it go and hit the refresh button. Your peace of mind depends on it.

Remember to breathe. Things that go wrong in life will be inevitable. You must find the stillness inside of you to be able to defy the storms of chaos. Make sure you stay in command of yourself. Find peace above dismay. Keep faith over fear, always. Wisdom over worry will take you further. None of this is simple or effortless. However - this life is a cycle of calm and chaos. Find the balance.

"Faith does not make things easier; it makes them possible."

The true testament in life is trusting what you don't see. There is so much working in your favor that is not visible to the eye. Having solid faith is quiet confirmation of all the things we cannot see. Develop trust in this setting and start believing before anything else. Faith - is strength and hope coexisting. By your courageous leap of faith, you are not submitting to darkness, on the contrary - you are embracing the light God has in store for you.

Keep faith alive.

We hear it often. "Just go with the flow".
There is a rare beauty in uncertainty.
Although, it can be intimidating and unsettling -
what the universe calls for will always land
precisely. Practice dismissing your worries
because it only interrupts today's bliss. Stop
exhausting yourself with thoughts that are only
living in your mind. Keep today full of strength
and hope. Whatever happens, happens. Be
grateful and stop worrying. It will be okay.

A new month is here, and you are ready
for new breaths and new opportunities. Make
this month a focal point for all things that bring
you happiness. Keep learning to love yourself,
unapologetically how you are. Surround yourself
with people who are motivated and inspired.
This is your time to convert into the best version
of yourself. Living happily does not mean
there are no difficulties, it means placing your
wellbeing before everything. Life will be full of
experiences. Have a positive attitude along the
way. Remember - things only seem impossible
until they're done. Go for it.

Time wasted is nonexistent. We dedicate
our time to what we believe in. Good or bad, no
matter the outcome, we live and learn. No matter
where you are in life, just remember that
everything you have lived has brought you to
this point. So, in essence, the only time that is
detrimental, is the time you spend worrying
about what you could have done differently.
Trust yourself. Be confident in your decisions.
Your path to happiness depends on it.

Keep your thoughts as happy as can be. Water them daily with positive affirmations. Furnish your mind with the wonderful joy of optimism. Things will not always go your way but don't allow that to discourage you. Continue to find peace in your faults. There is deep understanding in all our misfortune. Be patient with learning yourself as you grow older. Step into your everyday as if something amazing is waiting for you. When you're positive, good things will occur. Find ways to be in that space consistently. Be appreciative. Be grateful. Optimism will renew your faith in unimaginable ways. Trust it.

Always keep going. It becomes easy at times to become discouraged when we don't feel the support behind us. Keep in mind, the most important person behind you is YOURSELF. Stay the course no matter how many people don't believe in your journey. Keep embracing your destiny every day. I strongly believe we are always where we need to be. Remain vigilant. Remain patient but always stay productive. Believe in yourself.

The world will catch up.

I read a poem about happiness. It said
we are all already existing happy - it's just
dormant. Do not lose sight of your happiness.
We've all felt something that brings joy to our
spirit, and comfort to our heart. Stay where the
light is. This world has become a stage of
uncertainty and unfortunate events. It's easy to
be led astray and have your whole purpose
go awry. Stay inspired and lifted. Encourage
those around you to see the good in things.
Omit any loathing or resentment from your
heart. Be happy. Be grateful. Be yourself.
Your happiness will touch the world in
unbelievable ways.

All things done with sincerity and love will always return with an abundance of the same. Do not fret about other people's actions or how you think or feel they should pay you back. The ultimate reward comes from a deeper place, perhaps something not fully made clear. The most fulfilling indemnity will never feed your ego. It will instead, remit joy into your heart. Always give the best of yourself. Life has a way with karma. Everything necessary is always found within. Believe and trust all doors that open up in your favor. They'll always take you where you need to go.

In the development of your growth, continue to do your best with the intention of becoming even better. Stay aligned with your purpose and your truth. Do not be peeved by limited harvest. All good things founded in truth will eventually sprout as they should. Smile with gratitude. Laugh with abundance. Love with softness in your heart. Be a good human being - in that, you will unearth the gentlest truth.

PLANTING

Everything that you have carried through life, the gratifying moments against the downer days. It's all imperative to understand the primitive state of who you are becoming. Don't submit to the perception that your pain is out of place, frivolous or just a settled humdrum. Your inwardness is not meant to be abbreviated. Don't shrink yourself to make others feel comfortable. You matter - inside your finest moments and alongside your lowest. Live on every surface of your truths. There is beauty in a rose that grows from concrete. So, carry all your pain with a smile, and witness the finding of all its glory.

Sometimes fear will be the foundation to your greatest moments. When you feel afraid, do it anyway. Life's challenges aren't supposed to stonewall your success. They are there to aid you in the process of discovering your true self. Often times, the most difficult decision is to act. But once that commitment is placed, the rest is merely determination. Be not afraid of the leap - be more afraid of a lifeless spirit.

Live out your ideas. Breathe life into them. The beauty of creativity is that it's a never-ending mass of ideas, and the more you administer them with passion, the more you will bring them into existence. Imagine and create. Escape the repetitive pattern of routine and plunge into a pool of inspiration. Make the mistakes, learn readily, and push yourself to your maximum potential. Ideas will always be a normal thing. It will be your execution that sets you apart.

On our path to
success, we sometimes inadvertently
grow weary. We bulldoze through obstacles and
bustle through our heaviest days. We want to
win so badly that we refuse to pause for
intermissions. Our passion to succeed keeps us
unbending and set on the goal at hand. However,
it is also just as important to embrace the
standstill. It's imperative to find relief in
tranquility. Yes, the world is fast paced,
but we must learn to ease the tide, and rejoice in
the favor of quietude. The world may never find
muteness in the chaos, but your soul craves for
the hush of the day. Your destiny will always
resume, don't fret. Take a moment to be still,
and your heart will welcome peace.

The things that await you are beyond measure.
Have patience with what you have to offer.
Usually when things take time, it means it's
shaping into something that will harvest change.
Activate your faith and continue to
challenge the world, but also challenge yourself.
Accentuate the good things in your life. Fall in
love with what you do. The way you see and
do things is what makes you so unique. Forge
ahead and dig deep inside yourself. There is an
immeasurable force within you, fearful and
unstoppable. Tap into that realm and
embrace the infinite possibilities that live inside
you. It's all within you to reclaim your
greatness.

Be mindful of your journey in the macro but stay fixed on your next step. So often, we're troubled by the thought of making it to the end, and we bereave our field of vision. We cripple our progress by being so apprehensive. You can only ever take the steps that are in the forefront, so don't overwhelm yourself with futile things. Avoid the overhaul. Transformation comes over time. Little by little, one stretches far. Everything takes time. Keep following your heart and you'll always be closer than you were yesterday.

Don't die with your music still in you

- Wayne Dyer -

Do not allow your passion to be wounded by
conformity. Do not bend to the powers of
corporate America. Do not build dreams that
have no reference to you. There are a thousand
songs in your heart, ready to be heard. Do not
mute them for this shapeless world. There is no
degree of success in being well adjusted - make
a radical change. Always remember, a prison
becomes a home when you are the key holder.
Break free and begin living the life you dream
about.

Live an undying passion. Take steps that your heart will let you live with. Not every decision will be your best but make the effort to understand what each decision entails. Accept responsibility and hold yourself accountable with each mishap. Your successes and failures go hand in hand. Both will highlight the good and bad and bring you better understanding of self. Most importantly, no matter how sizable or modest your progress may seem, always be proud of yourself. You've come this far.

What a subtle death of the heart never given a chance to plunge into uncertainty. Your life should be filled with experiences, not just material things. We should all have stories to recite, not just things to boast about. The irony of exploring thoughtlessly is that we begin our travels to lose ourselves - yet, only to eventually find ourselves. Don't be afraid to flip the script. Don't be bound to the dull routine that discomfits your wanderlust. Keep your view towards the horizon. Your proudest moment awaits on everything that lies beyond.

You really have to know who you are in this world. You have to feel empowered when accepting every frame of your being.

Once you're awakened to your own worth, you will not feel superior nor underneath others, you will just simply be without the approval of anyone. Reverence your inner nature, acknowledge where you belong and also where you don't. Keep your ego safe and always in readiness to explore. So many amazing things will happen once you phase out seeking approval and validation. People will be drawn to you once you show the world that you cannot be shaken.

It goes without saying how many of us struggle with being happy. We have this idea of what happiness is supposed to enclose. We have expectations of others and ourselves that hold our most reliable truth captive. Validation outside of us is meaningless. People will cheer for you when they presume it to be worthy, and they will embalm you with hate the moment they see you're winning too much. All the external things are irrelevant. The most important conversation is always with yourself. Talk with yourself. Love yourself. Streamline the bullshit. Make it about you. No one else.

Our fears are implemented. They are clothed with doubt and worriment. The amusing aspect of what we fear is that it really never happens. Only when we put so much thought and attention to it, does it begin to be prominent in your life. Hold no bad conscience towards your fears. On the contrary, live in them, feel every corner of the fretfulness. How we face angst and misgivings ultimately outlines who we really are. Do not allow your fears to raise limitations on yourself. Always remember -Fear, may never pause death, but in acts of imprudence, it will most definitely stop life.

Life can be high handed at times. It can thrust in on us like a heavy storm. It will slender your vision if you are careless. Take control of your mind. There is always a widespread view. There is always something beyond the bounds. Do not miss the opportunity to see the bigger picture.

Fend off getting caught up in the specifics. Position your heart with purpose and understand that there is always capacity for greater thinking. It will always matter that you don't renounce your faith. Hold a genuine smile on your face, knowing that you are invariably a part of something so much bigger than yourself. Stop looking for the brightest light and learn to appreciate the gleam from broken fragments.

At any moment life can surprise us. It can breach our wellbeing and cause utter dismay. It can bring us to our knees and feel the bottom of the lowest. It can create turmoil in our soul and obstruct our vision for hope. Once falling down countless times you wonder if you can still get back up, you wonder if walking around with half agony and half hope is even feasible. The world is indeed full of ruined dreams, but in that fractured certainty, there still lies a contour of fairness. You see, life holds no accountability for the things we expect. At best, wrap yourself in the hope you live for. Live in it through and through. You will see - so much beauty still remains.

No step you take is insignificant. You've come
too far to let doubt fetter your
journey. No matter how modest the progress
may be, just keep going. Failures are the
intermittent roadblocks, not the end. Keep
learning and keep renewing your heart to
serve your purpose. If you're reading this, I pray
that extraordinary blessings feather a nest
in your life. I pray you continue to withstand
hardships with a bold face and a courageous
heart. I pray that compassion and love
furnish your soul, and that you may pass
benediction through your honest grace. I pray
that you believe in yourself no matter how the
world acquaints your presence. I pray that in all
the turmoil and suffering we will imminently
face, that we never lose faith in humanity. I pray
we always choose love.

Patience is passion tamed

- Lyman Abbott -

Take your time with yourself. Shift at your own pace and maneuver in accordance with what your heart is telling you. Ward off trying to follow suit out of fear. Impatience will shrink away any momentum that you bear. Allow things to happen naturally. Patience is the crowning quality. Great things take time to flourish. Stay calm in the process, bend your perspective and forge ahead with an unflinching spirit. It's okay if you're not where you want to be right now. You're going to make it.
Just breathe and keep going.

Be wary of self-doubt. Do not allow it to have the upper hand. It can create disorder inside your soul and make it very trying to find the peace you long for. Once you open that door, be mindful of how long it lingers. The irony of it all is that every time you doubt yourself, there are people who actually see the best in you. There is a strength often overlooked, which entails the capacity to skirmish that doubting voice that says, "I can't". Dismantle the fear of feeling inadequate. Undo the reluctancy that dwells in your heart. Embrace the threat of unsettled thoughts. Today, take a stand with your heart, and start wanting it more than you're afraid of it.

Do not allow yourself to feel inadequate with meager thoughts of feeling unfinished. Celebrate your journey, no matter how bounded you may feel. Small steps are still progressing, and you must honor your solid efforts. There is no shame when you know you are doing your best. Keep encouraging yourself. Keep supporting yourself. Remain firm in your truth. We as humans snarl up simplicity and we wonder why discontent comes so fluently. Life will always be a work in progress. Don't overthink it. Just be honest with your heart. That's the most intentional you can be, to witness progress, unapologetically.

Express yourself fully, without misgivings. Do not carry around the anxiety or the encumbrance of unspoken thoughts or feelings. Live emphatic. Live untamed and free. Live unashamed, unbending towards traditional action. Bring a voice to your intentions. Impeach all things that your heart is against. Uphold an intelligent point of view, never be rude or obnoxious. Speak boldly and lead with an armor of love. The right people will understand, and the right people will follow.

There will be days when this world may feel unsettling, muddled and maybe even a bit out of place. We begin to feel dispirited and dampened by the thief of joy. We begin to think we are not deserving of spanning joy in our heart. Joy is essential to our wellbeing and self-care.

Joy will thrust us into the most difficult situations, only to declare victory in the presence of challenging times. No matter what happens to you today. Embrace joy wholeheartedly. Smile. Define your place in this world before it defines you. Own your joy.

Share a sense of humor with someone. It
is a peculiar armor that helps preserve life and
helps inspire laughter during bleak times. Ease
the tension in every situation you can. Embrace
reality with a supple touch. There is an art to
living that has a lot to do with
mastering a saving sense of humor. Do not be
plagued by every pebble on the road. Find
merriment in your misfortune. Every time you
can come out of a troubled situation
with a sense of humor - you win.

I admire people who try. Those who see the probable outcome as failure do not balk at doing what's important to them. Only those who defy the odds will ever achieve largely. Always keep in mind, those who fall, but reclaim their power, will always be stronger than those who never tried. You will always learn new things about yourself on this journey of trying. When failing, admit it candidly, and try again. No matter what - try again. Disappointment only comes at the gesture of ignoring the bright side. Yes, the more you try, the more you may be scorned. But the less you try, the more you slay the possibility of embracing what could be your greatest achievement.

Hope. The most underestimated source to sustaining life. If you are dwelling in darkness, do not be so submerged that you forget to see the light of the stars. Even in our darkest times, there is an inhibited sense of betterment that is acquired. Hope, many times is born out of fear of something. We are so intimidated by the uncertainty, that we begin to doubt and start carrying colorless thoughts. You have to keep in mind, everything is impossible until it is materialized. For every bad thing in life, I firmly believe all good things lead us back to a balanced ground. Have hope, my friends.

Do not dwell on the losses. Always remember - with every loss, you're actually one step closer to winning. Never give up because of losses.

It is during our most challenging times that we come to understand so much about ourselves. All the time we get pressured by moments of uncertainty - those can be the most satisfying in finding achievement. The most beautiful thing about feeling tired, feeling like you have no more inside you to keep going - that is when you realize you are stronger than you give yourself credit for. We can outweigh our own expectations most of the time and that feeling is very rewarding. It becomes exhausting to think we have to figure it all out at once. Don't put that pressure on yourself. One day at a time. One breath at a time. Remain sound. The storm always passes.

It's easy to be discouraged. There are times when I want to relinquish all my efforts and just forget everything. But faith is a powerful blessing. Faith will thrust me to strengths I never knew existed in me. Faith will have me believe that hope can bring me back to life. It's time to let faith be bigger than our fears. Don't allow this world to dismantle your faith. It's in you - for moments of hopelessness and despair. You just have to wake it up when it's time to rise.

Things will often occur suddenly. Sometimes it will be at your lowest points right before you relinquish all your efforts. Good things are coming, and you have to remain keen on that belief. Don't be discouraged by the cloudy days. The sunshine is always around the way. You just have to make it there.

No matter what is happening around
you. No matter who you think is doing better
than you. Don't focus on that. Focus on your
own journey and worry about yourself. Most of
the time, people aren't as happy as they seem.
Don't always take it at face value. Don't be
deceived by what people post or say. Everyone
is at war with something. Nobody has it all
figured out but stay poised and always stay
genuinely invested in your purpose. You will see
everything beautiful that life has to offer.

We all define success differently. To me, success means making something from nothing and falling in love with it. Even perspective can be success in itself. You have to win in your mind before you can manifest true victory. Success is about escaping a poor mentality and finding ways to stay inspired every day. Success to me is knowing what you want and fighting to keep that fire burning at all costs. And every day that you continue to push and fight - then that, my friends, is what success is about.

True confidence will lift you to unbelievable heights. It will separate you from the rest. How you carry yourself will ultimately inspire or repress. Be someone the world takes notice of. Live courageously, breathe passionately, and no matter how foolish your dreams may seem, keep fighting to show the world why you believe in yourself. Be confident. Be kind. Be inspired.

Embrace the obstacles. The journey to greatness will never be still ground. You will confront troubled waters that will make you feel helpless. You will confront storms that will engulf your spirit. You will experience dark nights that feel discomforting. You will feel loneliness at its crest trying to break you down. So many things will try to impede your success. The major key is to remain present and amicable. Convert your disorder into discovery. Center yourself with optimism and hopefulness. Carry healthy thoughts that will assist you in your journey. Steer clear of all negativity that will annul your efforts. You have come too far to not keep going. Stay poised.

It's ok to restart, reset, and refocus. Life is a series of adjustments. We live and we learn. We all want to make it to the finish line. No matter what that really means, for now it means keep going. There will be trials and tribulations that disrupt your progress. Do not succumb to the excuses that make it easy to submit to failure. When you fall, rise again, and embrace the challenge. Have enough heart to always try again. Your daring spirit will reward you in many ways.

Do not create space for fear in your life. It will dim the light you have to give. Stay aligned with good intentions and trust every step you take. Fear is going to come but face it brazenly. Begin to understand that the things we fear actually become our limits. Do not let the temporary mind state of fear paralyze your spirit. Diminish all doubt and take charge. Walk through fear like your life depends on it. In many ways it does - because fear does not stop death, but it can stop you from living life.

Yes, this world has become a fast-paced environment, but having a waveless spirit that embodies patience - that is everything. There is a calm humility in the interval. Of course, we must never settle for complacency, but do not become discouraged by the setbacks. Have the patience and fortitude to always know that things will work in your favor. Have the confidence in yourself to know that you are not behind in life. Have the mindset that you are just "early in the process". Your dreams are guarded by your destiny. Continue on your journey. Life is on your side.

Mental peace comes when you are ready to break the links that don't bring any value to your life. Unhealthy attachments are not only perilous but can cause a lag to where you're trying to go. Your journey is too valuable for the intractable ways of life to cause deferment. Your shrewd decision making is imperative. Understand your purpose and walk that path with tremendous intention. Break free from negative settings and uninspired people. Your peace overall depends greatly on it.

"Calmness is the cradle of power"

- Josiah Gilbert Holland -

Remember to breathe. Things that go wrong in life will be inevitable. You must find the stillness inside of you to be able to defy the storms of chaos. Make sure you stay in command of yourself. Find peace above dismay. Keep faith over fear, always. Wisdom over worry will take you further. None of this is simple or effortless. However - this life is a cycle of calm and chaos. Find the balance.

Heartbreak is a necessary part of healing. We have to feel a little bit of disappointment at times to understand the true value of something. The irony is our hearts are made to be broken. But our hearts are also strong enough to overcome. Tomorrow is still a dream, so don't let today's battles cast a shadow on what's yet to come for you. Whatever stage you feel you're at now is not your final destination. There will always be better things ahead than what we leave behind.

Keep your head up. Show your spirit. Keep shining and keep igniting your passion for life.

BUDDING

Shed light into the darkest corners. Speak truth into empty words. Touch the ground firm with a presence that emits kindness.
Smile when it's hard. Laugh when it's even harder. Perseverance stems from flowers that flourish from the most vigorous dirt. How you grow from your circumstances will thrust you into the person you are meant to be. There is a forcible presence that you establish by just simply surviving. Never sell short the impact you have in this world. Big or small.

I promise you - you are significant.

Smile. You are not even halfway in everything you are meant to be. Trust in your journey. So many good things are coming your way. Life is a laborious road full of opportunity that will compliment your best days. And for the bad days, it will cause you to analyze and reflect on how you can be better. The best comes when you open the door to love, positive thoughts, positive energy, and most importantly - a good attitude.

Think of every misstep as a redirection to your most authentic landing place. When life tells us "No" that does not mean dismissal. It simply means a new course is aligning with your destiny. Just when you think your life is collapsing, it is also working behind the scenes on something better. A stage of refinement and rejuvenation will always come at the right time. Inquire as you move along on your path, new beginnings await. Morning will have its moment, without qualm. Allow old pieces of yourself to decay in the past and start embracing the dawn of a new day.

If something is truly important to you, then it will always be worth the uncertainty. Venture out with openness and determination. Even when the probability of failure is high, find amenity in trying. Start attracting everything you expect of your victories. Start becoming a reflection of all your desires. Begin to mirror all the things you admire. Explore more life and escape the familiarity of things you already know. The one who tries will always have the advantage. After all, your efforts may surprise you. So just try.

Be so loud with your happiness that sadness becomes daunted by your smile. The world needs more positivity. If you're fortunate enough to feel an abundance of it, please share it wholeheartedly.

It's important to be mindful and study every room you step into. However, do not allow the energy it pulls to influence yours. You will always be the proprietor of your own space. It's vital that you set the tone accordingly. How you initiate this will determine your relationship with others. Be poised, be framed with preparation, and deliver a smile worth embracing. Act first and lay the groundwork for your success. Keep in mind, you never want to be the person who adapts to the room, you want to be person who inspires the room.

Self-acceptance is a journey worth the stretch. It establishes space to find your truths. Unceasingly, aspire to be better. Be ambitious. Be eager. Respect yourself as you would want others to respect you. Being honest with yourself will deliver a sense of freedom that gasps for life. It's not your position to be everything to everyone. Always remember who you were before the disorder. Before they made you believe in who they wanted you to be. Self-acceptance is not about what you furbish with beauty, it's about growing through the toughest battles of life. You are worth this honor - and only when you take care of yourself, can you become a beacon of hope for others struggling to accept themselves.

Give prominence to the positive. In many instances, we find it so easy to dwell on the negatives. This will only cause unneeded burdens in your life. With a discerning heart, always look for the upside. Revel in the light of positivity, evade the darkness. Searching for unmitigated energy will ultimately mold your attitude. It will empower you and set fire to your deepest passions. Forge ahead with pronounced intention, and lucidity of the mind. Keep sowing your seeds with bewilderment in your heart. You may never know what may sprout from your doings but imagine what could - that is a wonder worth unraveling.

If you're doing your best. Be proud. Do not discredit your journey just because something doesn't round off. You are a thousand wars in and have yet been conquered. You have built an armor of perseverance and tenacity. Your purpose still radiates inside of you. When the sun fades for a while, learn to embrace the shadows. The world doesn't stay dark forever. Continue to walk with intention. Stay wild with big ideas, new adventures, and most importantly - joy in your heart. You're a survivor of your worst days and an eager soul for your best days to come.

Do not allow yourself to give up on curiosity. There is a unique existence that blends in the corners of wonderment. One can be in awe of life's framework when taking the time to comprehend just a little bit of mystery each day. Curiosity should be our first passion. It will graze us with the admission of finding new paths. So much adventure to look forward to by the one who genuinely binds their heart in everything. It's exciting to know that in the midst of daily routine, there exists another world in the backdrop of your mind. And all it takes is a bit of curiosity to unravel - what could just be your most fulfilling moments.

In so many ways we all long for significance. To
have an imprint in this world. To be remembered
by name and leave a meaningful
legacy. Many of us have ideas and thoughts that
have the budding desire to be seen and listened
to. Remain honest with yourself and brush off
the worry that your heart carries. Let
understanding settle in your soul as it reveals a
deeper love that you stand in need of.
Keep in mind - Having success is the inclusion
of value to oneself, but true significance is the
reputable value that you bring to others.

Wherever you show up in life - show up with love. Devote yourself to loving others, apply yourself to the community around you, and dedicate yourself to shaping something that delivers purpose and meaning to your life. Love bears value in all things. Love is the weight lifted off your jaded shoulders. Love is the light that calms the darkness. You will never be colorless if you are keen on love. Love for the sake of loving, drown in the depths of it. As we all perish and retire from life - people may forget most of what you have said and done, but they will always remember how you loved them.

There is a conversation going on inside all of us,
sometimes it's hapless thoughts that carry
a myriad of disquiet emotions, and other times it
can be an uplifting spurge of inspiration. It's
important that we cling on to the side of
cheer and encouragement. Do not be
discouraged by lack of support. The only true
fan club you have is yourself. Be your own
cheerleader. Serve yourself the love, respect, and
kindness you know you deserve. Be affirming to
your own greatness. No one is coming to hasten
your brilliance. Honor the potential you
have and begin owning the power that exists
inside you.

Always hold yourself to a high standard. You are a special kind of magic and not everyone is worthy of your measure. Outline yourself in the presence of those who relay love in its purest form. When you love yourself unconditionally, you begin to distinguish everything that makes you exceptional. Your place in this world is revered by the fire that continues to burn in you. You are far removed from ordinary. There is treasure in your soul. Your bones stretch with magic. Never accept the contrary. Your beauty glares in the darkest corners, and that's the thing with magic - It's undeniably breathtaking.

One thing this world does NOT need, is for us to be silent. Be brave enough to show up in all your truth. Give yourself the freedom to transmit all the things that matter most to you. This is a form of discovering peace. Be less inclined to say anything unless it creates positive reinforcement. Make sure good comes from the things you say. Be transparent and honest. We can formulate transformation in one another by raising our voice with compassion and truth. Do not yield to the scheme of silence. Roar with the loudest intention in your heart. Be deafening.

You are far from insignificant. You are worthy
of love. You are worthy of that conversation that
highlights your day. You are worthy of that hug
that shoves loneliness to the
ground. You are worthy of being heard when the
world is uproarious. You are worthy of the
affection that seals you with the gentlest
touch. You are worthy of happiness, that
paints your skies a placid shade of
blue. You are so deserving of all the goodness in
the world. You and all your complex layers will
always be worthy. Keep that close to your heart.

It's time you have an honest conversation with yourself. Clean out all the clutter that inhabits your heart. Get raw and unfiltered. Be courageous with yourself. Give yourself permission to tight grip your madness. You will never be able to serve others honorably if you keep lying to yourself. Do not enslave yourself with lies. Reaching the surface of truth will not always be easy, but it's imperative to begin accepting everything about yourself. Within you is the beginning and the end. Be who you are, unwavering, perseveringly, with a heavy hand. Your cloak will be lifted, and a fresh perspective will arise.

It's time to get excited for new ideas. Embark on the road of creative forcefulness. Write them down, imagine them, repeat them to yourself. Keep the ideas embedded in your brain. Believe in them without omission. Hoard them in your heart until it becomes an overflow of inspiration and desire. Liberate yourself from old ideas and old habits. Keep your mind open. Stay hungry and eager to learn. Edit your imagination and stretch your mind to captivate every creative draft you can imagine. Be a champion of new ideas. The world is starving for it.

There are no limitations in this life, only the ones you put on yourself. You are the barricade that resides between you and your dreams. You are your own worst enemy, that voice of doubt that brings concern to your heart. You are the rainy clouds that water down your vision. You are the disapproval that you see in your reflection. Stop swimming in small ponds and start creating something bigger for your legacy. Crack the limits, gap the boundaries and rift through life bold and confident. Master your intentions and push yourself into a new realm of courage.

Soak in the moment of the now and the glory it possesses. Become linked with the message you're receiving, and master layers of patience that will help you be ok with the unknown. Your attention should be aligned in things that can fetch a level of focus that will allow you to control what you can. This very moment is yours to shape. It is immeasurable, it is boundless, it is limitless. It is created of pure wonder and pursuit. Accept this moment right now fully and begin to witness a life changing grace of beatitude.

Your story is being written every day. Life stretches hope across our most arduous times. We must dwell on the possibility of what good can transpire. Believing in the ceremony of life, the breaths that mirror our most golden moments. There is an underlying joy in acknowledging what life has to offer. There will be rare moments that ignite our spirit and thrust our soul into magical feelings of elation.
Live freely for those moments.
Canvas your feelings of serendipity. There is power in governing our finest truths with a sense of wonder.

Your smile is so invaluable. It displays skyscrapers of hope and jubilance. It mirrors the most genuine parts of your being.

Protect your smile by all means. It is a decorative piece of your soul that the world must bear witness to. Your smile is a safe haven of love and compassion. It is radiance in human form. It is sunshine echoing from your inner core. The more you guide your smile resembling your highest truths, the more you will experience life in the most magical way.

Your heart is a divine map to every corner of your life. Adjust squarely, to the tune of what ignites your passion. Live with your heart wide open and unbarred. Love yourself without bounds. Get to know your spirit in its wholeness and in its blankness. You are so unique and brilliant. You are beautiful layers of bewilderment. You host a vast energy of inventiveness. You declare victory in the presence of unrest. You are exceptional. You are everything you believe yourself to be.

There is a calmness to the pain. There is a sound of healing that stirs the soul in times of misery. Your brokenness will serve as a gesture of hope. Because only in times of heartache and hardship will we adorn our most authentic self. Center your spirit when the walls of darkness surround you. Always remember - You are never shattering. You are always becoming.

A lot of us concern ourselves with
the risky things in life. The irony is none of us
will make it out alive. When you really think
about it - the epitome of life is risky. This world
is fast paced. Your hesitancy will put you behind
the rest. If it's lingering in your mind - take that
risk! History will favor the bold, it does not bear
in mind those who were timid. Stay afoot on the
road of uncertainty to alight yourself at the gate
of opportunity. Keep reaching. There should be
no qualms in the escape of routine to find a little
adventure.

You are deserving of life's beauty. You deserve
to be happy. You deserve every wonderful thing
that has already happened to you. You have
worked hard. You have been
resilient. You are incredible and
sensational. You must have the most respect
for yourself. Everything changes
once you realize your worth. You'll be in awe of
what you can attract by simply believing in
what you deserve. Allow yourself that freedom.

Just because you carry the hurt so well, so nonchalant and so unruffled, it does not mean it is yours to hold. Loosen that grip of all the things weighing you down. Allow yourself the admission to let go of the unnecessary weight. Once you do, you will sense a new beginning transpire. You will begin to soar higher than you ever have. There is a peace deserving of your gentleness. Dwell in that possibility. Dwell in the hope for discovery. Be brave enough to let go and have faith in what will be.

Carry optimism in your heart. It will decorate your life with hope and confidence. I am a firm believer that the hardest times in life are disguised as opportunities. Tough times build strong character. Accept every challenge that comes your way. Be brave in your heart and have faith in yourself. View optimism as a strategy to garner all good things in life. Be contagious with your optimism. Spread it like wildfire.

Just be happy for people
wish them success, be kind
allow them to be free in their spirit
without casting judgment
love those that need it the most
turn the hate into healing
learn from each other.
We can be better than this.

The world is thirsty for it.

Something to reflect on. You are a blessing to someone. Many times, you have offered a smile to someone that was sad. Many times, you have been a friend to someone who felt alone. Many times, you have said the right thing at the right moment. Maybe, all these times you never even noticed. But you must know that you are a light. Keep shining.

Give yourself more love.
Give yourself more understanding.
Give yourself more time.
Give yourself more patience.
Give yourself more faith.
Give yourself more opportunities.

Most importantly, give yourself more credit for surviving all the days you thought would destroy you. You made it.

Dwell on the assuring side of possibility. Find comfort in the warmest thoughts that bring you a sense of hope. There is so much more to come from your life. Keep dreaming, keep leading your highest self to the next level. Maintain a clear mindset. This world is your battlefield. Survive with grace. Do everything with a pure heart. Stand firm in your truth. No matter what life demands from you, always remember that you are great, manifesting with every breath. Remember that today.

Self-doubt can be haunting. It can steal your joy, but only if you grant it access to do so. What you believe in yourself is very critical to how you will progress in life. Focus on your strengths that magnify your maximum potential. Dwelling on your weaknesses will only impede your progress. The words "I'm not good enough" should never exist in the realm of your thoughts. Embrace the value that you possess. You've come too far to dim your own light. Know your worth and live your dreams out loud.

Find all the ways to keep yourself in spaces for opportunities. Most of the time, we create our own walls that hinder our progress. However, in the midst of difficulty and discord is where opportunity will find you. If you do not fend off all your excuses, you will suffer the misfortune of missed opportunities. After all, our lives in so many ways are defined by opportunities, even the ones we miss.

There is no lack of opportunity. We find it so easy to make excuses or to downplay our own potential. There is so much greatness living inside all of us. Most of us are scared to tap into it. Let us no longer be afraid and let's capture the very essence of what we are meant to be. We've all heard it before - we are our own worst enemy. It's not the world that holds us back. It's our own insecurities. The only walls that exist are the ones we imagine in our heads. Protect your thoughts. Guard your thoughts. We become what we think. So, think **BIG**.

Just as things happen for a reason, there are other things that have a reason for not happening. Have faith that the beautiful part of what is meant for you is right where it needs to be. Laugh through the bitterness. Smile through the tears. Always look for reminders that everything will be okay. No situation is ever wasted in life. Keep gaining insight and lean into new perspectives every chance you get. Be glad that things happen. No matter the outcome.

Today is a great day to start believing. Think about all the things holding you back and why you're so hesitant to take the next step. Most times we fear that we may fail. We become apprehensive. We become complacent and relaxed because it's a safe place to be. Great things don't happen in levels of comfort, they happen at the greatest heights when you're scared of the fall. But in that - you will grasp enormous strength. You will be overfilled with elation when you finally rise to your destiny. On the other side of fear, there is another world waiting for you and it's beautiful.

There is so much that our hearts carry simultaneously. There are times when we are healing and hurting at the same time. What this means is - we must offer more gentleness to the center of our being - our heart. The strongest hearts have lived a thousand lives. They have been scarred considerably, but in that - they have also established a foundation of hope. Keep your mind strong no matter how fragile your heart may feel. You are brave because you have lived. You are fearless because you have survived. Do not be wary - be everything good your heart wants you to be.

It's common knowledge that this world will never be perfect, and neither will we. Many things will not materialize in our favor. Many people will rarely act how we wish they would. Never grant that as an excuse to fall into gloomy or unfavorable places. Unfortunate events do not mean that everything is going bad, it really just means everything is going the way it's meant to be.

Allow things to run their course. Every season exhibits its own magic. Every story is distinct. Every person that exits your life, will clear space for someone better. Every obstacle you overcome will always make you stronger. You are grand in a myriad of ways. You have so much power - do not ever doubt yourself. Better things are always coming. Believe that.

Often times, we are hindered by the perception of ourselves. How we perceive the things we can do determines what we actually do. If you believe firmly in things you want to be great at, then you will be great. If you believe you'll never be good enough, then you'll never be good enough, at least in your mind. You see - our mind is a constant battlefield. You have to be equipped with the right ammo to overcome any doubt, fear, difficulty, and of course - all uncertainty. Win the war in your mind, and you will win in life.

Never play yourself small in a world desperate for your greatness. This world is a grand puzzle, and together we piece it to become what it represents. What do you want to bestow upon this earth? How do you want to be remembered? Do your actions represent your true self, or what you want others to think of you as? Desertion of oneself is a very dangerous thing. Fallacy will decorate anything beautifully, until peeled for what it truly is - untruth. Know yourself, unabridged. Believe in everything you are, and as you dwell in that truth, you will recognize your best self.

We are all for the most part
an untapped reservoir of unique potential. Do
not let the naysayers have their way. Do not let
uninspired people extinguish your fire. You are
meant to burn in your purpose. Your flames are
meant to decorate your path. Keep blazing with
unyielding intention. Stretch yourself to your
maximum potential. Become obsessed with
doing what you were created to do. You have an
incredible harvest waiting for your embrace.
Capture it.

BLOOMING

Today, be thankful. Honor your truth and brilliance. Have gratitude that your heart is not seized by greed and that your soul is not bent by envy. Today, let go of expectations, and embrace the celebration of all your victories. All the problems of the world, let them taper to the background and drain away. Today, fill your heart with the loveliness of all that is good. Life is a compilation of moments, and we truly never know just how impoverished we are, until our hearts are immensely thankful for everything we have. Today, grant yourself the grace of gratitude and wrap full heartedly the privilege to be alive.

Always live fully in your essence. Appoint eagerly and without reservations. Don't conclude with simply surviving. We are here to thrive, to admit passion with our own unique style. In good days, you will find joy. In bad days, you will learn uneasily. Do not be bound or tamed by time. Appreciate this moment right now, boldly, imperfectly and with all the uncertainty in the world. Don't fret over the unreeling force of aging, for It will always be life's greatest gesture of showing you that **YOU ARE STILL HERE**, and that will always be a beautiful thing worth celebrating.

Do you know how brave you are when you choose yourself? You must try undivided in all your humble pursuits. Choosing yourself will always be a modest courage worth ownership. Only go where your heart feels alive. The people you keep company, the books you delight in, the places you frequent. Fancy yourself in a circle of winners, but winners that want to see you win as well. We all have a story to tell and a unique service to offer. Master the form you want to show the world and love yourself enough to choose yourself.

Your peculiarity and uniqueness will always be the center of your comfort. Turn aside the reinforcements they try to impel on you. Avert from becoming a carbon copy of others. Take in arms all your eccentric ways and adorn every distinctive characteristic you possess. There is more strength and valor in being different. Emulating others is a fad that will soon fade into mental blankness. Leverage your singularity. Soften your spirit and feel at home with yourself. There is no one like you, and that will always be your superpower.

Perhaps the ongoing battles you are facing are just a testament to the resiliency that dwells in your heart. Perhaps, by surviving your greatest wars, it allows you to attentively exemplify great strength. You will begin to embody the magic of enlightenment. You will manifest great power in encouraging others to do the same. Success isn't just about what you do for self, it also encompasses everything you inspire in others. Never be ashamed of your story. It holds chapters that will be sung with hopefulness and clarity. Share it with the world.

Think of every morning as a rebirth. Take in the early dawn and the untouched beginning that it chalks up. The refined promise for hope. The new challenges that are eager to rise. There is a restored sense of purpose that is craving new solutions and opportunities. Do not carry yesterday's trash. Today, create new and breathtaking moments. Smile with grace. Walk with aim. Laugh with remedial joy in your heart. How fortunate you are to start another day, in the glory of all your truth.

So much makes you unique. At no time, undervalue what you bring to this world. Do not lessen your potential because others fail to accompany your joy. Everything different about you is worth honoring. It is worth celebrating. Be an artist that transcends their environment and looks to color the world offbeat. Do not be neutralized by labels and boxes that leave no room for perception. Being yourself is the one true gem that can genuinely elevate your life. Being different comes with some responsibility, but I find no better joy than to be anything but normal.

That smile that stretches across your face, that laughter that rings from your mouth. Those are highly colored reminders of your life's victories. You have survived internal wars, in the most intimate ways. You have survived battles that seemed like a hopeless case. You persevered through every threat that presented worriment or distress. The odds are always in your favor. The disorder you feel today will help devise the strength you need tomorrow. Every challenge is a roadway to opportunity. Don't be discouraged. Be inspired.

We are always blooming. Never be impetuous about how you flourish in this world. We all blossom at a different pace. Choose the things that align your heart with this notion. Keep in mind - flowers don't declare their maturation, they just simply undertake beauty as it flares. Don't concern yourself with being unseen. What's meant for you will still manifest accordingly. Continue to bloom gracefully, daringly, and emphatically. Even as you bloom prudently, just bloom. Acknowledge the beautiful unfolding of your becoming.

If you are fortunate enough to generate peace within, take it with you as you journey through your days. Share your untouchable armor that no man can harm. Demonstrate why the best fighter is never fazed by affliction. Share your longing to always treasure your supreme self. Help elevate others internally. Show them that negativity is below prosperity. Only deserted souls reside there. Claim understanding of yourself at the deepest level. Peace will never be a stopping place; it will always be part of who you are becoming.

Are you aware of your lighthouse? Be mindful, that darkness will never do away with darkness. There is a safe optimism in believing that there is a crack in everything. This is how light can find a way in. Be a bendable light in this world. Touch every dark corner with grace and wisdom. Shine on those who are situated in darkness, those who shudder at the shadow of death. Help guide their misgivings to the way of peace. The sun will rise and set, without pause. So, in your journey, climb with benevolence and compassion. Because love is not consolation, it is light, and that light is **YOU**.

There is such an honest feeling about being who you are. With no reservations, no doubts, and no apprehension. The only way to change the world is by being yourself. Be affluent. Be dauntless and gutty. Be all things that assemble the very essence of your being. Not everyone needs to understand your journey. You're not walking it for them. There are no rewards for conformity. Be yourself. End of story.

Take up space in this world. Dare yourself to be gutsy and capricious. Be courageous when it's difficult, be adventurous when time is fitting. Be spirited with good intention. Help people. Lift them up to their best self. Be kindhearted. Be gentle. Be gracious. Be thoughtful and understanding. Be a light that shines lucid. Be a voice of compassion. Be a touch of tenderness. Just be good in your heart, and take all the space in the world, so that you will not go unnoticed.

There is divinity in chosen timing. Meaning we are meant to go through situations that are anointed with purpose. They can be life wavering but also heart cleansing. They will teach us moments of clarity and feelings of thankfulness. Embrace the conviction that dwells in your heart. Begin to recognize everything that is possible for you. No matter how faint or subtle the desire is, just know you are covered with an amplitude of blessings. Honor your calling, it's how you become the most alive.

Be bold in your pursuit of
happiness. Be adventurous in all your endeavors.
It will be your unconventional ways of thinking
that will befriend your greatest
moments. Be daring, brave and foolhardy. The
mistakes and recklessness, allow it to happen
and be comfortable with the indiscretions. Every
day, we decide who we will be or not be.
Choose wisely, and always remember
- be courageous with your voice, unafraid when
listening to your heart, and firm in your strength
to live the life you've always wanted.

Believe unconditionally
- in yourself. Your ultimate superpower will
always be guarded by what
you claim in your life. You are enough, and you
carry a myriad of greatness in your realm. You
are capable of encompassing many wonderful
victories. Remain confident in your journey and
discharge all doubt from your heart. You are
going to make incredible change, and you will
flourish in your many truths - so long as you
remain disciplined in your growth. Keep living.

Think about all the days you've survived. All the wars that disrupted your waves of placidity. Everything that came to dismantle your spirit, but to no avail. Think about every blemish that touched your soul in the course of dark times. Every corner of worry that fuddled your being. **IT DID NOT WIN**. You are a survivor of intimate wars that could have ravaged the very essence of your foundation. You survived every day leading to this very moment. Be proud of your victory. There will never be a more triumphant feeling than that of surviving your worst days.

There will be dark times. There will be moments of dolefulness. There will be nights that seem unending. There will be many things that will come to disrupt your peace. Do not become discouraged by life's impropriety.
There is a unique sense of humor we must carry tenderly at our side. Smile in the face of uncertainty. Caress the darkness. Show life that no matter what skies it brings you, you know how to make something beautiful of it.

Throughout your journey in life, you will
unearth transitional stages. There will be
moments that shudder your core, and others that
will be rounded with gentleness. Be present in
all of them. There is a sense of salvation with
changes that flourish within your spirit. No bad
day will last forever. Every good day is well
deserved. Adjust gracefully, and you will see
good things come to fruition.

Each day, rise with intention and gratitude. Decide without delay how you want to feel about your day. Get centered and set. Positive vibes will come when that is the focal point. Apply your energy in the most creative way to see the essence of your magic. Never underestimate the power of peace that comes with accepting who you are. Always love yourself for all your dauntless efforts. You have so much to benefit. This world is your map. Make it worth the trip.

You've come this far in life, and you continue to strive. You have been against all odds and have survived rugged and raw. Don't let anyone discredit what you've been through. You deserve the sun just as much as the next person. Live free with love in your heart and truth in your voice. You are worthy of every precious moment that life has brought you. Embrace your good fortune and continue to live inspired.

You can be waiting for flowers your whole life and miss out on the beautiful garden you could cultivate yourself. Moral of the story - don't wait for happiness to find you. Find happiness within yourself, and you will never feel like you are owed flowers - you will simply be grateful that you are standing on soil that can bring about your own.

To the mothers - you are the light that captures beauty in its purest form. You are sunshine that breaks through the storms of difficulty. You are the smile that comes from overcoming obstacles. You are the joy that swarms over darkness. You are compassion in human form. You have a love that burns deep and honest. You comfort worry in unsettled waters. You heal with your touch because you bear superpowers. Your warmth is felt on the coldest nights. Today we honor you - in all your bravery, in all your strength. We celebrate your legacy of love.

Let today be a beautiful reminder of how great you are. How you are meant to do amazing things. How unmatched you are because you are unique in every sense. You are worth more than you believe. Do not fear uncertainty. You can achieve anything that you set your mind on. Have a beautiful day, and please keep believing in yourself.

No one ever knows all of what it takes to be you.
It's important to celebrate yourself. Be proud of
every piece that makes you who you are.
Continue to see the best in yourself. Continue to
speak highly of yourself. Keep allowing your
light to shine bright. Celebrating yourself is a
form of self-love. Find comfort in approving of
yourself. You will see beautiful things manifest
in your favor by doing so. You are worthy of
celebration today. Embrace it.

Something I read this morning -
"You will never lose what is for you"

With that being said - give your heart into the
things that stir your soul in the happiest way.
Without attaching yourself blindly, find comfort
in loving deeply. The right things will always
find a home in you. I have the strongest faith in
believing that I will always be right where I need
to be.

Resilience will give birth to a type of strength that you won't know you have, until that is the only thing left in you to breathe. Life comes in waves, and it's so easy to be dragged through the worst. However, through that pressure, through that adversity and misfortune, a new version of you will be born. One that you will be proud of. Because there is nothing more beautiful than a heart that keeps surviving.

Kindness to me - is making an impact in a subtle but moving way. It is wanting to see someone smile, to see someone happy, to *SEE* someone - period. This world can be harsh and unkind. It can breach your innocence to the core. Believe in the power of kindness. It can change the world immensely. Be a light. Be a smile. Be that gleam of hope someone needs to not feel alone anymore. The side effects of this include - happiness, excitement, compassion, strength, and connection. Please - go be kind.

The love you give today, you deserve it too. The smile you give today, you deserve it too. Do not make the mistake of selling yourself short. Never. Every time you accept anything less than you deserve; you are guiding others on how to treat you. Know your worth. The people of this world will plot against you. Make sure you don't ever see yourself through their empty eyes. Have the courage to be who you are. Value yourself.

Fight for your happiness. When you are happy, you will make others happy too.

The joy of overcoming the dark times will put a genuine smile on your face. You will heal from hurt, you will heal from pain, you will heal from all the darkness that surrounds you. You will soon realize how extraordinary things will turn around and begin working in your favor. Most times, these gloomy days lead to the most sunshine you will ever behold. Be patient and keep faith conscious in your heart. Please believe - Blessings are on the way.

We can easily become discouraged when our days are bleak and shadowy. It's hard to smile when the sun is clouded, and our joy is withheld. The challenge is to overcome the tenacious roads that lie ahead, finding strength in places we never knew existed. We become stronger by all things that try to bury us. We must rise above every beating, every debacle, every collapse that tries to dismantle our spirit. We are survivors, and we are planted in truth. May our hearts speak with no reservations, and our actions hold power to embrace every hilltop towards our destiny.

I believe it is imperative for us to find joy in the now. Times of old will always hold a special place by virtue of the memories they retain. but those moments had their place in time, a beautiful nostalgic remembrance. Also, thinking too much of an unknown tomorrow can be a cloaked thief in the night. Let nothing steal the joy of today. The beauty of now, and the plentiful moments that you may convey to the universe. We are all beautiful beings in an endless realm of uncertainty.

Don't spend so much energy trying to convince people of things. Whatever it is you're doing in life - **JUST EXECUTE**. Some will cheer you on, and others will wait to see if you fail. Leave the reactions in their court. Focus on what you need to do to make sure you're advancing to the next level. Stop talking and get to work. Success is yours.

It's ok to manifest in silence. The world doesn't need to know your every move. Follow your own compass. Like a seed that grows quietly, fruitfully, and abundantly. Focus on your moves rather than your announcements. Move with purpose. Always remember, a fool will speak for the sake of speech. A wise person will use their silence as power. Know who you are.

Some people will never be able to grasp the type of energy you bring. They may not yet be at the level you are at. They may not have the depth or capacity to comprehend the magic that shines within you. Surround yourself with those who know your value. I promise when you begin to acknowledge your own importance and self-worth - you will move differently, and the world will know.

If life ever gifts you special people and beautiful moments, don't be surprised by the notion. Embrace it at full strength because you deserve it.

It's a special feeling to be around those people that never look to dim your light to brighten theirs. Those that push you towards greatness. Those that help you believe in yourself in times that you find it difficult to do so. Those people are such a blessing, and they deserve all the recognition in the world for being genuine spirits. If you're fortunate enough to be in the midst of this blessing, cherish it, hold on to it. Little do you know - those people are saving you every day.

How often do we speak of beauty? And when you do, how often do you leave yourself out of all the beautiful things you have to say. Let this be a reminder today -That you are beautiful. You are amazing, and you are always worth more than you believe. The world, as hard as it can be, will always try to harden your soul. Don't allow it to take away from the beauty that you have to offer. You have a place in this world. But you only make it better by showing up as your authentic self. Always be you, unapologetically.

Continue to choose all the good feelings in life. Choose to love, and your heart will be filled with the same. Choose to find peace, and your life will mirror those intentions. Choose happiness, and your world will become that happy place for yourself and those around you. Choose the good things in life. Choose what makes your heart smile. You will be happy every time you do.

Embrace every part of who you are. We're not meant to be perfect. We all have imperfections, and we all struggle with certain things. Be honest with yourself. Be brave and confident in your uniqueness. Find yourself and have the courage every day to shine in your own light.

Be vigilant in your journey. Pay attention to how the universe directs your destiny.
Don't be careless with the signs. Every day is a step closer to where you're supposed to be.
Remain disciplined in your actions. Be inspired, but also be patient. We all have a purpose. Once you find it - live it with all your heart.

If there is something to chase, then let it be happiness. Search for it. Find it. Explore it. Live profoundly in every magical part of it. The journey should be exciting. The uncertainty of things should inspire you to be comfortable with being uncomfortable. There is an undeniable amount of joy once you start becoming the person you are meant to be. Embrace it with your all.

That thing that makes your heart
vibrate. That thing that makes you smile
openly. That thing that feels right where you're
supposed to be. That is your passion. That is the
beautiful feeling of affinity. Protect it with your
all.

Promise yourself that you will be brave. Promise yourself that you will be fearless in achieving your dreams. Remain focused and committed. Have the audacity to venture into the unknown. Promise yourself you will always live a life that is true to you. Life is an adventure, and despite all the risks that it entails, you must preserve a daring spirit. Never underestimate the essence of your personal promises. Once you discover the nourishing joy it brings to your heart - you will want to make all the room you can for it.

Be genuine. Be presentable. Be of value. Hold yourself to a high standard. Walk with purpose. Be an example to those that hem in your presence. Speak wise. Smile with a sense of joy. Laugh with the sound of gratitude. Be present in moments that call for it. Do not compare yourself to others. Do not ever disfavor your self-worth in that manner. You will always be unique. You will always be your own beauty. Bask in your own greatness. You are worth every ounce of it.

As cliché as it may be, never stop dreaming. Dream big. I promise you - your dreams are well-founded. Never allow angst to cover your heart with worry. The space between reality and your dreams is microscopic. If you have a vision and you wholeheartedly believe in it, you can make things happen. You are capable and you are worthy. Keep conviction alive in your heart and start taking the necessary steps to achieving all of what life has in store for you.

Be irrational - be illogical - be foolish.

Dare yourself to dream!

STAY
Inspired

"And the day came when the risk to remain tight like a bud was more painful than the risk it took to blossom."

Anais Nin

For

Jose Vela

Ivan Lara

Alvaro Abarca

Aaron Martinez

You are free.

Made in the USA
Columbia, SC
27 January 2025

52451144R00150